D1647955

Contemplative Prayer

Contemplative Prayer

*Praying When the
Well Runs Dry*

Joann Nesser

Augsburg Books
Minneapolis

Cover design: Laurie Ingram
Cover image: © Christopher Pattberg / iStockphoto.com
Book design: PerfecType, Nashville, Tenn.

Library of Congress Cataloging-in-Publication Data
Nesser, Joann.
Contemplative prayer : praying when the well runs dry / Joann Nesser.
        p. cm.
ISBN 978-0-8066-9065-0 (alk. paper)
1. Prayer—Christianity. 2. Contemplation. 3. Spiritual life—Christianity.
I. Title.
BV210.3.N47 2007
248.3'2—dc22
            2007028216

The paper used in this publication meets the minimum requirements of American National Standard for Information Sciences—Permanence of Paper for Printed Library Materials, ANSI Z329.48-1984.

Manufactured in the U.S.A.

11 10 09 08 07 1 2 3 4 5 6 7 8 9 10

In gratitude
for all the saints
past and present
who have accompanied me
on my spiritual journey

Contents

Preface

O God, you are my God, I seek you.
My soul thirsts for you;
My flesh faints for you,
As in a dry and weary land where there is no water.

PSALM 63:1

My eighteen-month-old daughter was sitting on the kitchen floor playing with the pots and pans. The sun was shining in through the south and east windows. The room was flooded with light. As I stood in the doorway taking in this scene, it seemed to me that there was another Light filling my kitchen. I felt a gentle Presence in the room. There was nothing earth shattering or mysterious about it. I thought that this is the way it should always be. We should always have a real awareness of God present in the ordinary, every day events of life. I wondered why most of us do not.

This wasn't the first time I had struggled with the question of our lack of experiential awareness of God. I had begun to take my faith life seriously shortly after high school. At that time I questioned whether or not all the things I had learned as a child in Sunday school and Confirmation were really true. Did they fall into the same category as Mother Goose? Questioning like this drove me to the Bible to look for some evidence of truth. I can't say I found what I was looking for, but I did decide that I wanted to believe in God and seriously practice my faith.

In my early twenties, I met a woman who had converted to Hinduism in her search for meaningful prayer and relationship with God. As a girl from a small town in the Midwest, this both shocked and jarred my Christian thinking. How could she do this? And yet, if I were honest, I had to admit that I admired her ability to meditate and her commitment to spend time in silence. I had to confess that I could not pray for fifteen minutes without a flood of distractions and even boredom. I wondered why we, who profess a relationship with a living God, don't have more *experience* of that reality in our lives. Consequently, I set out to learn more about prayer.

For help I went to a local Christian bookstore where I purchased a small book of daily devotions. I bought this book because it was half priced, but I believe it was God that placed that little book in my hands. This was my introduction to the contemplative tradition, as the little readings in the book were all taken from the great classics of Christian spirituality. The authors spoke of their relationship with God in a very deep and intimate way. They seemed to have an immediate, felt experience of God in their lives. They spoke of love, warmth, tenderness, guidance and revelation. They spoke of God, and to God, with love, passion and mystery. This stirred in me an even greater desire for a deeper prayer life and drove me to seek answers.

I had never heard this kind of language in reference to my relationship with God. In fact, I don't think I would have spoken in terms of relationship at all but would have referred to faith or belief in God. The writers of my devotional book seemed to know God like people who lived with Jesus intimately every day. As I searched for answers, I found that I wasn't the only one who didn't know about intimacy with God. I found that many people were highly suspicious of experience or emotions when it came to God.

I found that in the Western hemisphere, our emphasis has been on science and technology for generations. Our culture and environment shape and influence our worldview. We come to our spiritual life with a worldview and presuppositions that affect both our approach to God and our response to God. Western Christians were reared in a rational culture based on ideas inherited from the period known as the Enlightenment in the eighteenth century. Under the influence of the Enlightenment, it came to be believed that only that which could be proven by the scientific method was true. This has deeply affected the value we place on emotions and feelings as well as on the arts and literature. Spiritual experience was looked at as mere superstition. Anyone who professed an *experience* of God was suspect. They were thought to be heretics or even mentally ill. Many were even burned at the stake as witches. The rational scientific approach affected all of life.

Our rationalistic culture also has affected how we conceive of church. As an example, in my search for a deeper spiritual life, I talked to my pastor who then referred me to the choir director, the Sunday school superintendent and the youth pastor. They all invited me to get involved. I was soon singing in the choir, acting as a youth counselor, and teaching Sunday school. No one mentioned anything to me about prayer or personal spiritual growth.

Churches typically respond to spiritual growth in this way. When new members join the congregation we immediately try to get them involved in some activity or service project. We think of our spiritual leaders as those who are very active. Spiritual growth is demonstrated by becoming the head of a committee or serving on the church council. Pastors often work sixty or seventy hours a week—and we expect it. We have done relatively well at encouraging people to serve, but we have not done well at encouraging (and facilitating) personal experience of, and a love relationship with, God as a vital part of spiritual growth.

Because most denominations rightly stress that we are saved by grace and not by works,[1] there is a reluctance to talk about spiritual growth, spiritual formation, and spiritual disciplines in Protestant churches. There is a fear that people will think they can earn more of God's love and favor by doing such things. That fear keeps many from exploring traditional spiritual practices that open the door to personal spiritual growth. Instead of inviting people to practice spiritual disciplines, we teach. We offer more and more workshops, seminars, and classes believing that if we are learning we are growing. One pastor told me that traditional Protestant spiritual formation was good teaching. Besides furthering this attitude, most clergy have simply not been prepared to offer help in personal spiritual growth because seminaries have focused on academics and offered little in the way of training in spiritual formation.

In the middle of my dilemma, God sent an angel, a Roman Catholic sister who invited me to a Cenacle Retreat Center. My first retreat was total culture shock. My past experience with retreats had been of long and frequent speakers, get-acquainted games, too much coffee, and late nights talking endlessly about trivial things. We were usually housed in dorm cabins of six or eight bunk beds like teenagers. We brought sleeping bags and nothing was furnished but a well used mattress. The bathroom down the hall was designed for, and obviously used by, large groups of teenagers.

This was different. When I entered the Cenacle, a host who guided me to a small guest room greeted me. It was simple but tastefully furnished. This was my very own room. For a young married woman with three little children, it had been a long time since I had that much private space. After getting settled in our rooms we had a light supper and met together for orientation and to share our expectations of the retreat. We then were to be silent until the close of the retreat. The private room and the silence gave me permission to relax and just *be* with no need to make small talk.

For short periods throughout the retreat, we gathered in the chapel for a simple teaching on prayer and were given several scripture texts to pray with during our time alone. I learned that silence and scripture meditation were very much a part of Christian tradition and history. There are no words to describe the profound affect the silence had on me. My prayer became a time of being together with a very personal friend. I began to experience the nearness and love of God in the depths of my soul. The deep needs of my life that, in my busyness, I had been able to brush aside, began to surface and I began to experience God's inner healing and renewal.

Later I learned that personal experience of God, solitude, silence, and meditation were a part of Christian tradition that had been largely lost as science and psychology began to play an important part in society. The great saints of the Church wrote about being "in love with God" and being empowered by this love to bring renewal to the Church and world of their day. Until the age of science and rationalism, contemplative prayer was considered normal spirituality. Spiritual direction and personal formation, once the center of pastoral ministry, lost its place to clinical pastoral counseling. Without this centerpiece of personal formation, in recent years serious God seekers have been looking to Christian history in order to find ways to meet today's needs. They have discovered that the early Church understood God as desiring a real and intimate relationship with us—a relationship centered in mutual love. This is the center of Christian faith and life that enlivens and enriches our worship and service as they flow out of this profound experience of loving and being loved by God.

I believe that all kinds of prayer are helpful and that God answers prayer. When we come to God with our concerns, our petitions and intercessions, God's power is released into the situation in real and profound ways. There are many good books written about this type of active prayer that should be a part of every Christian's life.

What I have found over the years, however, is that there comes a time when the desire to pray in this way changes, particularly for those who have been serious about their spiritual life. Many, if they are honest and dare talk about it, would say that they have lost their desire to pray; that they are tired of their prayer lists and feel guilty because of the way they feel. They haven't lost their desire for God but they have lost their desire to say prayers and participate in many of the spiritual practices that have served them well for years. Because of our lack of knowledge of spiritual growth, most Christians do not understand that this dryness is an invitation from God to enter into a new kind of prayer.

After many years of attending silent retreats and practicing my own prayer, I like to say I accidentally began to lead retreats on prayer and became a spiritual director. Fearing I might be leading people astray, I sought out, and was blessed to find, Shalem Institute for Spiritual Formation. Shalem gave me the space and encouragement for my own deepening as well as the grounding I needed for leading others.

Through the privilege of leading retreats and listening to others talk about their prayer, I have found that the thirst for a deeper relationship with God through prayer is universal. We all bring a certain worldview, a certain amount of cultural baggage, but in the end God calls us to transcend these and experience love, intimacy, healing, and wholeness.

Based on these many years of seeking, finding, listening, and growing, I offer here what I hope will help those who long for a spiritual life beyond simply going to church and saying their prayers. I would like to give some understanding of the dynamics of the spiritual journey and offer ways to move through the transition from dryness and the loss of desire for active prayer to knowing God in the depths of one's being. For those who have faithfully prayed petitions and intercessions and long to know where to go from here, I am offering a few different ways to think of prayer along with some practices that will be helpful as you move into a more contemplative spirituality.

My thanks go to all the great saints who opened for me the possibility of knowing God intimately through their writings on contemplative prayer. My thanks also go to my spiritual directors and the friends who have walked with me over the years, especially Jeanette Bakke, Tilden Edwards, Dick Beckmen, John Ackerman, all the wonderful people at Christos Center for Spiritual Formation, and all those who have shared their spiritual journeys with me in spiritual direction. Thanks to my editor, Gloria Bengtson, and to Susan Johnson and all those at Augsburg Fortress who were involved in making this book a reality, especially Henry French, who made my words say better what I wanted them to say. And last, but certainly not least, my thanks go to my very patient and supportive husband, Joe, and our family.

A Different Way to Think about Prayer

And this is eternal life,
That they may know you,
The only true God,
And Jesus Christ whom you have sent.

JOHN 17:3

Our ideas about prayer have been so damaged by our rational way of thinking that sometimes I think it would be good if we had another word for prayer. As a starting place we could think of prayer as communication. Communication happens in any relationship, including our relationship with God. It happens at any and all times, not just in our set times of prayer, although this is where we give our total attention to communicating with God.

On the spiritual journey, prayer is our way of communicating in our love relationship with God. This is not just any relationship, but a *love* relationship with God who is *Love*. Just as any love relationship requires times alone together, we need such times in our relationship with God.

1

As we journey together, our communication grows and deepens. As it grows and deepens it also changes. There is no rule that says we must pray in a certain way at any point on the journey. We should always pray in a way that is life giving. As we pay attention to what is happening inside when we pray, we will be invited to the kind of prayer that is right for where we are on the journey. The Holy Spirit leads us. We only need to follow. Our communication is not about correctness or performing, but about listening and responding as in any good relationship.

In this love relationship with God, prayer is our communication and our conversation with the One who loves us and who desires us to love in return. Prayer is so much more than making requests. It is a sharing of our spirit with the Eternal Spirit who has created us. In this relationship, as in any relationship, the partners share their deepest feelings and their most precious secrets. God desires to hear our deepest feelings and thoughts, and will share deep feelings and thoughts with us.

Scripture often refers to our relationship with God as that of a bride and bridegroom. This is the kind of intimacy God desires in our communication. A friend once referred to the time of prayer as a trysting place with God. A trysting place is a place where two lovers meet. This metaphor sheds some light on the kind of relationship and communication we should have with God.

When we enter a life of contemplative prayer and relationship with God, we enter a trysting place. For some this can be rather frightening. We can feel very vulnerable and anxious about where this will lead and what will be required. We need to remember that God is a God of love. God never requires more of us than we are ready to receive. God has created our personalities and will come to us in ways that are attractive to our personality. God never forces us; rather God invites us to follow. God never imposes or intrudes into our lives. Whatever takes place in our spiritual lives we know that all is by grace, by God's unmerited favor, a free gift out of the abundant goodness and love of God, and not to harm, control, manipulate or hurt us in any way.

Every person is unique. We are all different and the way we relate to God, the way we are being shaped and made new, will be uniquely ours. Of course, there are similarities with the experience of others that can help us understand our own journey but each person will go through experiences, changes and responses to God in their own way and in their own time. We all grow in different ways according to our personal needs and responses. The Holy Spirit will guide us when we are listening to the still small voice within. We are all invited to grow and deepen into the unique and special person God has created us to be. Spiritual growth is the unfolding of this special person as we continue on the journey.

The Spiritual Journey

For surely I know the plans I have for you, says the Lord,
plans for your welfare and not for harm,
to give you a future with hope.
Then when you call upon me
and come and pray to me,
I will hear you.
When you search for me . . . with all your heart
I will let you find me, says the Lord

JEREMIAH 29:11-14

The best way to describe what happens when one makes a serious commitment to spiritual deepening is that it is like starting out on a journey. On any journey we depart from somewhere and we have a destination. There is movement from one place to another and experiences that we must go through in order to get to another place.

This dynamic of spiritual growth and movement is often spoken of as a journey because as we continue to seek God in prayer there is an element of discovery and of change. There is an on-going revelation of God and of our true selves. Just as pioneers or explorers have set out on a journey to some new uncharted territory, when

4

we begin to seriously seek God we find we are entering uncharted territory. We will encounter mysteries of God and of ourselves that we have never known before. We will discover the wonders of a God who loves us more than we could ever have imagined. We will discover the uniqueness of ourselves as we are healed and loved into being by God who continues to create us through the power of the Holy Spirit.

We may travel through uncharted territory and experience places that we have never seen before, but we have a traveling companion, the Spirit of Christ, who knows the way. The point of departure may be different for each of us but our common destination is healing, wholeness and intimate union with God.

When we speak of spiritual growth it is easy to fall into an achievement mentality. We begin to feel that we should be more spiritually mature than we are or that we should be praying in some other, more advanced way. It is important to remember that we are all unique and we all experience things in different ways and at different times. Spiritual growth is not a straight line, but a spiral—we are ever returning to places where we have been before and coming to new understandings.

We are never going to be perfect in this life. As long as we are human we will make mistakes. We will do or say the wrong things or make poor choices. That is the human condition. We can live our lives in complete freedom knowing that God knew before we were born who we are, what we would be like, and what we would do. God knew the mistakes we would make, yet loves us and has chosen us to be lovers and friends forever.[2]

This was an incredible revelation for me. I always felt like I had to be perfect: a perfect wife, mother, community citizen, church member. Of course, I failed all the time. I rehashed everything I did, feeling guilt and shame and that I simply wasn't good enough. Even though I knew I was forgiven in my head, it wasn't until I encountered the real love of God in scripture meditation and prayer that I knew forgiveness in my heart.

It may take years for us to experience the freedom to live every day without feelings of guilt or shame but it is not because God is placing that on us. It is because in our brokenness we are unable to experience this freedom. As we continue in our prayer and grow in awareness of God's love, we will be healed. The point for us to remember is that our life is not going to be like another's and there is no correct place to be in our spiritual growth. As long as our heart's desire is to seek God and to be all that God has created us to be, wherever we are on the journey is the right place to be.

When I speak of the spiritual journey I am speaking in the classic sense of growing awareness and union with God and God's will. The spiritual journey takes place within the soul, in the deepest center of our personal being. It is not about gaining intellectual knowledge, but rather the knowledge that comes from love of God and of self.

In the beginning stages of the spiritual journey most people relate to God intellectually. We decide we want to be serious about our spiritual life and we want to know what we must *do* for God. We try to *learn* all we can by reading the Bible and other books about God. We may begin to attend church and get involved in service to others. We change our behavior to *doing* good works and may drop off activities and friends that we deem sinful. Nevertheless, we may not be aware of any interior relationship with God save for an occasional *sense* of God's presence. This often happens during a worship service or in nature but is not commonly experienced in the ordinary events of daily life.

The spiritual life at this point is very active and external. It is about *doing* with little experience of the value of just *being*. The spiritual life in the early stages consists of busyness. If there is prayer it is active petition and intercession. There is little consciousness of the supernatural experience of God that transcends our intellectual understanding or control. We are not very aware of our traveling companion, the Holy Spirit, who guides the way, nor are we aware that it is normal for our spiritual life to change as we grow.

We may be content to stay in this place for a long time. As time goes on, something often happens in our life that will bring about these changes. Something makes us reach out to God in new ways. It may be a personal crisis such as serious illness, the death of a parent, a problem child, loss of a job, a divorce, or other life transition. Sometimes it is unanswered prayer that moves us to reach out to God in new ways. These are normal life experiences.

Whatever it is, it causes our previous understanding of God to fail. We realize we aren't in control. We may question our old beliefs and cry out to God for answers or we may throw ourselves on God's mercy realizing our dependence and need for God in new ways. It can happen at anytime but from that point on we become aware of a different understanding of God and new dimensions in our need for God. Our old ways of praying and relating to God simply don't work anymore.

This is a normal transition in spiritual life. There has been so little guidance in the area of spiritual growth, however, that most people do not know of this dynamic of change and do not understand that there is far more to the spiritual journey than the practices they did in the beginning. They often try to continue the spiritual practices and ways of prayer that were helpful when they were setting out, but now they find them dry and empty. No one has pointed to the deeper dimensions of the journey of prayer.

The experience of dryness and emptiness is an invitation to move into unfamiliar territory. A few may turn away from God at this point, experiencing the dryness and emptiness as the absence of God. Others, out of fear of losing their familiar God, continue to function in the same old way denying the internal changes that are taking place within them. Those who accept the invitation, however, will begin to experience a more interior relationship with God. This is an invitation to more reflective and listening prayer. It is an invitation to pay attention to God, an invitation to a growing contemplative awareness of God. It is also an invitation to silence and solitude.[3]

Along with the experience of a more interior relationship with God, it is common to feel both unconditional love and a new sense of inner peace in spite of the seeming inability to pray with words or even read the Bible. Often, in accepting this invitation to an interior experience of God, we find we have more questions than answers. There is a longing to be with God but when we are alone and desire to pray there are no words that answer the desire. We discover that what we truly desire is nothing more than to sit quietly and just *be*. This is the beginning of a more contemplative way of praying and relating to God.

In the chapters that follow, I have included suggestions for reflection that will help you absorb and experience what you are reading. Practice and experience are important; they help to ensure that what you are learning will become heart knowledge as well as head knowledge. Rather than just reading about prayer, as you follow the suggestions in each chapter, you will *experience* the inner reality of prayer. For these exercises you will need a notebook to use as a spiritual journal. Kept faithfully, your journal will become a helpful tool for your journey and growth in prayer.

Keeping a Spiritual Journal

Write the vision;
Make it plain on tablets,
so that a runner may read it.
For there is still a vision for the appointed time;
it speaks of the end, and does not lie.
If it seems to tarry, wait for it;
it will surely come, it will not delay.

HABAKKUK 2:2b-3

Your first exercise is to begin a spiritual journal. A journal is an ancient tool used by serious God seekers throughout history as a way of being in touch with both God and themselves. As modern examples, think of the journals of Dag Hammarskjöld, Mahatma Ghandi, Dietrich Bonhoeffer, and so many others. b

When you write in your journal, remember that it is for your eyes only. When these great saints wrote their journals, they weren't writing for the benefit of others. They were writing for their own growth and understanding. A spiritual journal is a tool to help you recall what has been happening in your prayer. There is no need to write profound thoughts or to say the right words.

Whatever feelings, thoughts, and emotions you have, express them in your journal. Be creative. If you like to draw or paint, and it helps you to express what you are experiencing, then fill your journal with drawings. You can also write your own psalms or poems or hymns.

You can copy into your journal the words of a scripture text, a poem, a song, or other writing that touches you and speaks to your own spiritual journey. In my journal you will find quotations from American poets, Emily Dickinson and Mary Oliver, and many others. They don't have to be particularly religious—they just have to speak to you and your experience. I have used songs from U2, Van Morrison, and the theme from the movie *Notting Hill*, just to name a few. The point is that whatever you write or draw or copy into your journal should be a window to God *for you* in the present moment.

At times you may feel very near to God; you may feel a deep sense of peace or love. These feelings should be written about and described in your journal. At other times you may feel empty, dry, alone or sad. Write about these feelings; explore in your journal what prompted such feelings. This practice helps us get to know ourselves better.

Monastic reformer and mystic Teresa of Avila would say that self-knowledge is important in order to grow in our knowledge of God. Reflecting on what some of the ancient writers would call our interior movements help us to notice the *still small voice of the Spirit* breathing within us. We begin to notice what draws us near to God and what pulls us back.

Writing what we notice when we are quiet and alone helps us to become more sensitive to the inner movements that are happening inside us all day long. We are then able to notice more clearly how God is guiding us in our daily lives. Reading back over our journals gives us a broader perspective of what is going on in our lives, of how we are reacting to life events and how closely we are following what God is inviting us to become.

Reflection

To begin your journal, write about your hopes and dreams for your spiritual life as you enter into the spiritual practices and new ways to pray that you will discover in this book. Remember, all of your life is your *spiritual* life so include your vision of what a full and meaningful life for you would look like. Deep down inside each of us is our true self—the self that we are in God. Our true self is often masked by the false self, the egoic self that has been shaped by life circumstances, by culture and society, by those who have taught us, and by the choices we have made. Who do you think your true self, your *self in God*, might be, and how might your true self be different from the egoic self that you and others think you are? Reflect on these things and write them in your journal. You will find it a good beginning to a new chapter in your spiritual journey.

Prayer in the Beginning of the Journey

Ask and it will be given you;
Search and you will find;
Knock, and the door will be opened for you.
For everyone who asks receives,
and everyone who searches finds,
and for everyone who knocks,
the door will be opened.

MATTHEW 7:7-8

As mentioned earlier, when you start out on a journey, you have both a starting point and a destination. You begin somewhere and you are going somewhere. At each stage of the journey you need to be focused on where you are between the starting point and the destination.

The focus during the initial stages of the spiritual journey is on getting to know God. When you have just set out as a serious seeker of God, determined to practice prayer, you will most likely experience God as being outside of yourself. You may feel that

God is up in the sky or in the church, especially near the altar. Feelings of nearness to God are intermittent and usually come when you are attending worship services, singing a hymn, receiving Holy Communion, or at prayer. At other times you might have a vague sense of God's presence when out in nature or when listening to beautiful music. You will most likely have little or no sense awareness of the *indwelling* Christ. When you pray you have the feeling of praying to God who is *out there somewhere.*

We desire to draw near to God. Certainly God is near to us but we don't have an intuitive, inner awareness of God's presence. In our efforts to get to know God, we read the Bible and other books, we talk with people, we attend classes and listen to sermons. This is normal when we first get serious about our relationship with God. We seek to know God through our senses and our intellect. Our feeling, our experience, our longing is that of yearning to *know* the Other and to have the Other *know* us. In time we will learn that knowing God requires much more than our intellect; knowing God is *knowing in love.*

It is very important at this place in the journey to share honestly with God in prayer. God may seem awesome and distant, but Jesus is the friendly face of God. We often feel more comfortable addressing our prayers to Jesus. The discovery that Jesus has promised to answer our prayers, to teach us, to relieve our weariness and heal us is new and exciting.

Sharing our real and honest feelings about our lives and our needs is a very necessary part of deepening our prayer and awareness of God. Many of us have not done this kind of praying. We say our memorized prayers and we pray petitions and intercessions for ourselves and other people, but we do not talk in a deeply personal way to God about ourselves. You need to know that it is not at all selfish to pray for ourselves in this way. It is part of the *getting to know you* time in prayer.

As a spiritual director, I have known many who are afraid to show God their anger or lack of trust, thinking it isn't right to feel this way about God. Others hold back honest feelings about family members for the same reason. I have known many women whose lives have been turned completely upside down when their husbands retire but they won't say it to God because they think their feelings are wrong. To move into deep contemplative prayer one has to be completely honest in prayer.

This is also the time when we want to bring all our requests for others to our friend Jesus. Most people feel relieved that at last they have found help for those situations where they have felt so helpless. We don't have to have some special formula for this kind of prayer. Jesus has promised to hear our prayer. He understands our pain, our questions, and our heart cries. Here is someone who wants to listen to our hearts and doesn't tire of hearing our troubles.

At some point in the journey, most of us realize that life has wounded us in many ways. We feel broken and fragmented. This brokenness is a hindrance to our experiential awareness of God. Whatever causes us to feel inferior to others, whatever has made us feel rejected or lonely, whatever causes us to hold back in our relationships with people will affect our relationship with God. As we relate in prayer to God who loves us and calls us beloved, and as we are honest about our hurts and brokenness, we find healing for our many wounds.

This might seem like an odd place to begin contemplative prayer but, in my experience, when we start taking time to be alone with God to listen and reflect, long buried thoughts and feelings emerge that we didn't know were there. They have been hidden for years under layers of busyness and often denial. This can be a scary time for some and it is important to know that it is a very natural occurrence. By paying attention to the memories and feelings that surface, we can look at them, bring them into our prayer, and allow God to heal us and fill us with love and forgiveness. (We'll say more about this in the chapter on spiritual direction.)

Many years ago, after I had begun to give intentional time for prayer, there would be times when a sudden feeling of love would come over me and fill me with a deep sense of being loved, and even precious, to God. This awareness of God's love for me began a long, slow process of healing life-long feelings of inferiority and low self-image. None of us have perfect parents and the people we have encountered along the way have not been perfect either. Even the most loving parents and siblings and friends are human beings with human weaknesses.

Most often through no one's intentional fault, we have received hurts and wounds that have made us feel unloved or unacceptable. Who hasn't suffered with some form of low self-esteem or shame? It is God's desire that we be healed of our broken, wounded selves. If we have fears or hurts from relationships with our parents or other authority figures, it will affect the way we relate to God.

Often, if you have had a harsh, strict, or legalistic parent, you will transfer the same fears, shame, and ways of relating to your relationship with God and will not experience how much God loves you. Negative experiences with the church, or people we have trusted, will affect our ability to trust God. These experiences cause us to hold back in all relationships, including our relationship with God, throughout our lives. As we enter more deeply into a contemplative relationship with God, we will find healing of these deep wounds and will come to experience God as both friend and lover.

As our relationship with God deepens, we grow in our sense of self-worth, self-trust and in the knowledge that we are loved. Our resistance to God diminishes as we allow the Holy Spirit to love us within. We become more able to love others as we learn to love ourselves. As we experience inner healing through prayer we are more open to receive God's love and our relationship with God becomes more intimate and experiential.

Past sins also cause us to be afraid of God and hinder a growing relationship with God. Today we often don't like to use the language of sin and yet, for each of us, there are patterns of behavior, things we have done and continue to do, things we have not done and should have done and continue not to do, things that we are ashamed of and want to change. Over and over again, we fall into the same old ways of being and behaving no matter how hard we try to be different.

Even when we hear that God forgives us, we can't seem to forgive ourselves. No matter how many times we hear the words of forgiveness, we continue to carry the same old feelings of guilt and shame. Being told that we are forgiven doesn't change the way we feel inside, and these feelings become an obstacle to our freely relating to God. As we open ourselves to God in prayer, however, we begin to experience a sense of forgiveness that goes beyond words and that heals our guilt and shame.

Reflection

Sitting quietly for a few moments with eyes closed, reflect on what things seem to be a hindrance for you in your relationship with God. What experiences with parents, authority figures, or others have caused you to hold back in relationships? What past behaviors have caused you to have a hard time both accepting God's forgiveness and forgiving yourself?

Try to imagine yourself sitting with Jesus in a favorite place. Imagine yourself telling Jesus about these experiences and how you feel about them. Sit with Jesus silently for a while and just listen to what he might say to you in response to what he has heard. Quietly speak your response to what Jesus has told you. Then, gently open your eyes and write your reflections in your spiritual journal.

Experiencing God's Presence

Because you are precious in my sight,
And honored, and I love you . . .

ISAIAH 43:4

Whether or not we have been Christians all our lives, most of us have little conscious awareness of our relationship with God until something takes place that causes us to experience our own limited nature, or until something happens to make us realize that life is not something we can control. Asking serious questions about life usually produces questions about God and becomes an invitation to a deeper relationship with God. If the invitation is accepted, a conscious dialogue with life and God begins, a dialogue driven by our desire to truly *know* both God and life. With this desire and dialogue comes the growing *experience* of a conscious *awareness* of God's presence. This comes as a feeling of warmth or love inside. We may feel a deep sense of being loved, of being special and cared for.

When we experience this conscious awareness of unconditional love, we may feel a sense of unworthiness or sorrow for our
sin. For example, when the prophet Isaiah had a vision of God in
the temple, he exclaimed: *"Woe is me! I am lost, for I am a man
of unclean lips, and I live among a people with unclean lips; yet my
eyes have seen the King, the Lord of hosts!"* [4]At other times we may
simply have a wordless inner *knowing* or sense of Presence much
like that of the Hebrew poet who wrote: "Be still, and know that
I am God."[5]

The Gospel of John tells us that the Triune God will come and
make a home in us.[6] Through some great mystery the Trinity dwells
in each one of us. There is no one who can be closer to us than God.
Only God lives within our very own soul. We are never left alone.
Jesus tells us that he loves us as much as God loves him and that we
are his friends.[7] He promises us that he is always with us.[8] Again,
in his high priestly prayer, Jesus prays that *"the love with which God
loved him would be in us and he in us"*.[9] Whether we are aware of it
or not, we live in relationship with a living and personal God.[10]

All of these verses speak of an indwelling relationship and love.
God invites us to participate in a relationship of love and friend-
ship when we are called to follow Jesus. Not only are we invited to
love God, but also throughout the scriptures God expresses love
for us. God tells the Israelites that they *"are precious in my sight,
and honored, and I love you."* [11] God also declares, *"I have loved you
with an everlasting love, therefore I have continued my faithfulness to
you."*[12] These are just a few isolated verses. Throughout scripture
we find verse after verse telling us of God's lavish love for us, and
God's desire that we return that love.

To live as a Christian, that is to live with trust in God's gracious forgiveness, acceptance, and redemption, it is not necessary to have these deep feelings of interior love and Presence. However, it seems to me that a God who expresses such love as we read about in scripture and in classic devotional literature would also desire us to have a conscious awareness of that love.

I have often thought of the bride and bridegroom metaphor that is found in scripture and liken it to my relationship with my husband. What would our relationship be like if I told him that I loved him but had no feelings, emotions, or experience of that love in my life? And what would it be like if I told him I had no expectations of feeling love from him either? I could tell him that it wasn't important because we have a marriage certificate that says we are married, and so we neither need to feel anything for each other for ourselves nor do we need to feel the other feeling anything for us. This would make no sense at all, nor would it make either of us very happy. We need the intimacy and mutuality of deep communication, feelings and emotions in our relationship with each other. Could we need any less in our relationship with the God in whose image we were created?

It would seem that God knows what will make us happy. We live in an intimacy and love-starved world. Years ago a popular song declared that, "What the world needs now is love, sweet love." This is even truer today as people go from one broken relationship to another.

God invites us into a love relationship unlike any other. Only God knows us intimately in the very depths of our being. Only God knows our hearts, our hurts, our needs, and our desires. No other being can penetrate our soul to its very core and fill it with love, comfort, and peace.

Although feelings and emotions are not always present, it doesn't mean that God is not present. Jesus said that he would never leave us nor forsake us and that he would always be with us.[13] Theologically, we know that God is present with us but most of us don't notice that presence. In the beginning of the journey, we often have a feeling of separation or distance from God. Our *experience* becomes one of seeking or longing for God. This longing itself is already prayer, placed there by the Holy Spirit who dwells within us and prays in us and for us.[14] The yearning for God will be with us throughout our journey calling us deeper and deeper. The feeling of longing does not mean that we need to be somewhere else on our journey than where we are in order to be near God. God is already and always near and our longing is to experience God's presence more and more deeply. This deep longing is what keeps us going deeper.

All through our lives we will have both feelings of distance and closeness to God but, particularly in the beginning of our conscious seeking, we more often experience a sense of distance or separation. Even though we may know intellectually that we are in God, we may not feel that way. Our whole spiritual life is one of seeking to bridge that distance and draw closer to God. Our spirit longs to draw near to God's Spirit. This longing is actually a gift that causes us to want to pray, read scripture, or be together with others who know this God we long for.

As in any personal relationship, there is a desire for closeness and intimacy. Classic devotional literature often uses the term *union*. We long for union or oneness with God. This is not the oneness of the self's annihilation, but the oneness of two participating beings, Creator and creature, becoming one in love and purpose.

In our human relationships, we often find that when people deeply love each other, when they do things together and value the desires of the other, over time they often become like each other. For example, think of the many older couples you have known who, after many years of marriage, begin to look and act alike. Often they use similar language and gestures when speaking and may even finish each other's sentences. This is similar to our relationship with God. As we relate together closely and spend time together getting to know each other deeply, we begin to share a desire for the same things. The Eastern Orthodox go so far as to say we are being "divinized;" we are being made divine.

As we grow in relationship with God, we become more and more intimate with God and grow to be like Christ.[15] This is the work of the Holy Spirit. It is not something we have to strive for; it is the natural transformation that occurs as we continue on the journey. Just as in the beginning of our journey we may feel separated and distant from God, as we gradually mature we will more often feel oneness with God.

Reflection

Sit quietly for a few moments. Close your eyes. Reflect on your experience of God. When have you *felt* God's presence? What was that like for you? By thinking of that time, can you go back there in your memory and recall (perhaps relive) the experience? Ask God to help you. Sit with the experience for as long as you can.

Gently open your eyes. How did it feel to go back to that experience in your memory? The ability to recall your past spiritual experiences can be a helpful tool in your prayer life. Write your reflections in your spiritual journal.

The Indwelling Christ

I ask not only on behalf of these,
but also on behalf of those who will believe in me
through their word,
that they may all be one.
As you, Father, are in me and I am in you,
may they also be in us,
so that the world may believe
that you have sent me. . . .
So that the love with which you have loved me,
may be in them,
and I in them.

JOHN 17:20-21 & 26b

As stated above, until now you may not have been aware of your traveling companion, the Holy Spirit, who guides you on your journey. God lives in us. The journey takes place within. As we enter this interior relationship with God, we find that the Holy Spirit is no longer simply the third person we confess in our Creeds but the very dynamic and active Presence of Christ within our own soul. We are all dwelling places of God. We are *never* alone or apart from God.

We teach little children in Sunday school to sing, "Come into my heart, come into my heart, come in to stay, come in today, come into my heart, Lord Jesus." Yet most of us don't really believe it. Even though our theology says that the Spirit of Christ dwells within each of us, we don't really believe it. We are more likely to believe the theology of the popular song, "God Is Watching Us." The God in this song is a God "in the sky," a God far off, watching—and presumably judging—what we do.

This watching God is not experienced as either intimate or immediate, and therefore, only knows what we need if we ask specifically, and will only answer requests made in a specific way. Most of us simply do not live as though God is truly present with us in the world and also present within our own souls.

Many scripture passages, however, remind us that we are filled with the Holy Spirit. A careful reading of the book of Acts will show that it was the common and expected experience of early Christians to be indwelt by the Holy Spirit. In Romans 8, St. Paul clearly tells us: "*But you are not in the flesh; you are in the Spirit, since the Spirit of God dwells in you,*" and "*When we cry, 'Abba! Father! It is that very Spirit bearing witness with our spirit that we are children of God . . .*" [16]

This is why we experience the spiritual journey as an inner journey. In prayer we communicate with God's Spirit who is active *within* us—not outside us—healing and renewing us, and transforming us into the image of Christ that is the goal of the spiritual journey. In contemplative prayer we open ourselves to the transforming love of God. We notice the interior movements of God's Spirit inviting us to grow and deepen, and revealing to us our true self that is created in the image of God.

It is essential that we realize that we are indeed indwelt by the Holy Spirit and that the Holy Spirit can and does communicate with us in the deep center of our soul. When we are in listening prayer, we are listening *within*. Many of the ancient writers on prayer encourage us to *turn within* when we seek to meet with God for God dwells in our very own heart. I believe it is essential that we believe this and trust that the indwelling Christ will be revealed to us if we are open and paying attention.

Reflection

Sit quietly for a few moments. Think about *where* you experience the presence of God within. Try to locate your *sense* awareness of this Presence. For example, you may feel the presence of God in the place of your heart, or perhaps in your breathing, or perhaps in your forehead. Some may even feel a sense of God's presence throughout their entire body. Wherever you feel the sense of God's presence within you, focus on that place. Stay with the experience as long as you are able. Gently open your eyes. Try to continue to be aware of this inner Presence while you write about your thoughts and feelings of the indwelling Christ in your spiritual journal.

Spiritual Growth

I pray that according to the riches of his glory,
He may grant that you may be strengthened
in your inner being
With power through his Spirit,
And that Christ may dwell in your hearts through faith,
As you are being rooted and grounded in love.
I pray that you may have power to comprehend
with all the saints,
What is the breadth and length and height and depth,
And to know the love of Christ that surpasses knowledge,
So that you may be filled with all the fullness of God.
Now to him who by the power at work within us is
able to accomplish
abundantly far more than al we can ask or imagine,
to him be glory in the church
and in Christ Jesus to all generations,
forever and ever. Amen.

EPHESIANS 3:16-21

Spiritual growth has to do with opening ourselves up to the grace of God that has already been poured out for us through Christ. It is not about trying to win God's love. God's love has already been given. We are simply learning to be open to and receive the love and grace that has been given.

Theology that stresses being saved by grace and not by works[17] should grant us great freedom. All too often, however, it becomes a stumbling block to spiritual practices that can help us experience that grace. Many times when speaking to a group of people in my own denomination, I have encountered reluctance to talk about spiritual disciplines because of the fear that it takes away from God's generous grace. It is important for us to remember that we are already God's children. God's lavish love has already been poured out for us. Spiritual practices help us more deeply *experience* that grace and love. As we experience more fully the grace and love of God we are able to rest more fully in that love. Prayer becomes more quiet and peaceful. We become more childlike and more Christlike in our love for others.

When I speak of the changes that happen in our prayer, I am not speaking of what we *must do* in order to belong to God. I am simply *describing what happens* as our prayer grows in response to our longing for God. I am being descriptive not prescriptive, describing *how* people most commonly *experience* the relationship we have been given by grace. Sometimes we are like Lazarus bound by guilt, shame or fear.[18] Spiritual disciplines or practices put us in a place where we can hear the freeing, unbinding, already spoken voice of Jesus. That has nothing to do with works righteousness.

I am describing the common dynamics of spiritual growth. There is no spiritual ladder of perfection that we must climb to please God, but there are normal stages of spiritual development that are experienced when a serious person seeking God responds to the invitation to participate in the intimate love that is present between ourselves and God.

It is important to know these foundational things because what we believe about the spiritual life will shape the way we experience God and the way we pray. To understand our responses to God we need to understand the dynamics of our relationship with God as it grows and changes. Our part on this journey is to seek, and be open to, God. God's part is to heal, deepen, and renew us.

Our tendency is to want some evidence that we are maturing. When we have that mentality, we set ourselves up for disappointment because we don't always recognize our own growth. Real maturity in the Christian life is living in the moment and, like St. Paul, *"forgetting what lies behind and pressing on to what lies ahead."* [19] We can't do anything about what happened yesterday. To enjoy the fruit of God's forgiveness, it is important to let go of the past. We can't change anything. We can only accept forgiveness and live in the moment in gratitude for what we have received. Teresa of Avila would even tell us to forget self and concentrate on God. [20]

Reflection

Sit quietly for a few moments. Close your eyes and think of the way children are with a loving parent. Imagine a little child seeing her mother coming to the play yard. The child has smudges of dirt on knees and arms as well as around her runny nose. Seeing the mother, the child runs to give a big hug and kiss without being conscious of how appealing or unappealing she might look. How does the mother react? Does the mother push the child away or scoop the child up in her arms? Jesus tells us to become like little children. What does this mean to you? Write your reflections in your spiritual journal.

Praying with Scripture

I will meditate on your precepts,
And fix my eyes on your ways.
I will delight in your statutes;
I will not forget your word.

PSALM 119:15-16

Because we are so filled with inner noise and words, it is very difficult for most of us to become quiet enough to listen to either God or our own deepest inner thoughts. We may give ourselves a time of silence to be with God and then quickly discover that creating external silence is easy compared to silencing our internal noise.

Usually our thoughts randomly run around our minds without our thinking much about where they come from. Many of the ancient writers on prayer would say that our inner person is made up of intellect, memory, imagination, and will. When we experience something, all these inner faculties are activated in a moment. For example, when we see something or hear a sound, our intellect will immediately make a judgment as to what it is; our memory will recall something that it reminds us of; our imagination will make a picture of it; our will decides what we want to do with the information. In short, a seemingly uncontrollable train of thoughts, feelings, images, and emotions fills our minds.

A useful practice that can help you to understand this dynamic is simply paying attention to where your thoughts and feelings come from. What triggers your thoughts and feelings? For example, think of a situation where you had to walk into a room where people were already standing around talking in small groups. What happens inside of you if a few people look up at you and then turn back to their conversation without acknowledging your presence? Your intellect registers what happened, your memory might recall another instance when this had happened before, and you begin to have the same feelings you had then. Your imagination might begin to tell you that these people don't like or accept you or that they think they are better than you. All of these thoughts are random; you may have little control over them, and much of the "information" you are processing may not even be true.

When you decide to spend time alone and in silence with God, the same type of random thoughts take over. They are like a community in anarchy. It is difficult to listen to God when there is so much inner activity.

It reminds me of the years when our children were small. It seemed that whenever I wanted to have a serious conversation with someone the kids would suddenly become particularly disruptive or noisy. For example, if I made a telephone call to the doctor when all seemed quiet, as soon as I picked up the phone there would be chaos. Someone would suddenly be digging in the refrigerator or picking a fight with a sibling, and all of it seemingly out of my control. When I needed silence, I learned to give the children something to do that would give me a space to do whatever I needed to do.

A traditional practice for learning to bring order and control over our thoughts is *scripture meditation*. We do not want to completely close off our thoughts but we do want to give them something to do while we open ourselves to God. We can give all our inner faculties something to do by taking a short passage from scripture and *entering into it* through our imagination. It may be difficult at first, but in time and with practice the inner faculties are quieted down more easily. When this happens we will be ready to move on to a more simple type of meditation.

When we enter into scripture meditation our focus should be on God and not on the words themselves. The purpose of the meditation is to open ourselves to God and not to *study* the scripture passage. This is not an intellectual exercise but a devotional practice to help us listen to God. We are seeking to relate to God in an intimate way and to learn to be open to God's love and presence in our daily lives. Meditation is a tool to help us set aside our distracting thoughts and focus our attention.

Because it is God who has initiated relationship with us and invited us to intimacy and love, it is God who chooses the agenda for our times of meditation. It is not up to us to make something happen or to *get something* out of our meditation. Our responsibility is to take the time to be there, to meditate and so open ourselves to God's loving action. Our role is to be present, approach the text in a prayerful manner, and listen. You may find it helpful to read the passage out loud, a phrase at a time, closing your eyes and "listening" between each phrase. God is always faithful to meet us, whether we are aware of it or not.

These meditations are a way of getting to know God's character and God's faithfulness to others down through the ages. One also begins to experience God's personal love for us as individuals. As St. Teresa of Avila and other ancient mystics would say, we gain *loving knowledge* of God through meditation. It is not a knowledge that we can grasp with our minds, as God is ultimately incomprehensible, but it is a knowledge we gain with our hearts. Ephesians 3:18-19 says: *"I pray that you may have the power to comprehend, with all the saints, what is the breadth and length and height and depth, and to know the love of Christ that surpasses knowledge, so that you may be filled with all the fullness of God."* Loving knowledge of God is the fruit of meditation.

In the sixteenth century, Ignatius of Loyola, a leader in the Counter Reformation, founded the Society of Jesus, a very large and powerful Roman Catholic religious order. As a method of spiritual formation and ongoing renewal, Ignatius developed the Spiritual Exercises, a method of praying the scriptures—particularly the Gospels—that continues to be popular today, not only with Roman Catholic religious, but also with both Catholic and Protestant laypeople. Using these Exercises, one begins by asking for God's help and presence, and then prays with a portion of one of the Gospels by using the imagination to *enter* the text. One imagines being in the scripture scene with Jesus and whoever else is in the scene. For example, one listens imaginatively to the sounds, tries to smell the smells, and feel the warmth of the sun, or the sand in one's sandals.

This can be a very enjoyable and eye-opening way to read scripture. Through your imagination you can readily experience being in particular passages of scripture almost as though you had really been there. Simply read the chosen text, close your eyes, and begin to imagine what it looks like. What do you see? What do you hear? What do you feel with your hands, feet and other parts of your body? What can you smell? Can you taste anything?

Next watch the people in the scene. Notice their actions, their expressions, and their responses to what is happening. Listen to what they are saying. Then try to *enter* the scene yourself. Who are you? What are you doing? What is your response to what is happening? Do you speak to Jesus? What do you say? How does he respond? What is God saying to you through the text that relates to your life right now? After you have completed this reflection, conclude with whatever your response is to God in prayer with your own words.

This type of meditation can leave you with memories of scripture stories as though you were actually there. Of course, we know that what we imagine is not *fact*, but God can speak through our imagination and this form of meditation is a wonderful help in making the scripture stories meaningful to us in new and fresh ways. The Holy Spirit will speak through our meditation on scripture to teach us about ourselves, to heal us, to renew us, and to help us with questions or problems we may have in life or in our relationship with God.

My first experience with this kind of scripture meditation was at the same Catholic retreat center where I first attended silent retreats. I had been accustomed to reading many chapters of scripture during my devotional time and had done Bible studies and Bible memorization for years. My spiritual director told me, "Joann, you have read that book, why not let it soak in." This began a profound change in my understanding of scripture.

Scripture is meant to speak to our hearts. For several hundred years our institutional approach to scripture has been a rational, critical form of study. This fails us because we can never *prove* the existence of God or who Jesus was, nor can we experience God personally by reading and rational, critical study alone. Our intellects can help to *lead* us to God but we can only *know* God or Jesus through personal encounter. Our knowledge of God grows not through study but through *"faith working through love."* [21] We gain *loving knowledge* of God through prayer, meditation and contemplation. Just as what we experience is supported by what we learn intellectually, what we learn intellectually should be supported by the loving knowledge we gain through our hearts. We need both the intellect and the heart.

Reflection

Sit in your sacred space. Prepare yourself for the meditation by simply breathing deeply, watching your breath, and letting go of busy thoughts. Try to *feel* the center of your soul where Christ is present. When you feel attentive, read the passage (see below for suggested passages). For this type of meditation use a scripture story that forms a mental picture. Begin by reading the passage slowly. Listen carefully to the words. Try to imagine the scene in the story. Try to *feel* the climate or weather of the time and place, *listen* for the sounds, *smell* the smells, *taste* the tastes, etc. Put the Bible down and *be* with the scene. *Watch* what is happening. *Notice* expressions and attitudes of the players. Next, try to enter the scene yourself. Where are you in the scene? What is happening? How are you responding? Listen to what is being *said to you*.

Listen. . . If your mind wanders, bring it back to the scene. As you listen, pay attention to any thoughts or responses you are having. Savor them. If there is something you would like to say, perhaps a question you would like to ask to anyone in the scene, then say what you need to say and listen for their response.

When you feel you are finished, quietly return and thank God for meeting you in your meditation. Write your thoughts in your journal. Remember the journal is to help you deepen your relationship with God and to get in touch with your true self. It is not meant for anyone else's eyes. If you are self-conscious about what you are writing, you will not be honest and the journal won't be very helpful.

Here are a few suggested texts for exploring this form of meditation: Matthew 12:46-50; 18:10-14; 19:13-15; Mark 1:35-37; 5:25-34; 14:1-9; Luke 1:26-38; 24:13-35; John 4:1-26; 5:1-15.

Another Way to Pray
with Scripture

Come to me, all you that are weary
and are carrying heavy burdens,
and I will give you rest.
Take my yoke upon you and learn from me;
for I am gentle and humble in heart,
and you will find rest for your souls.
For my yoke is easy, and my burden is light.

MATTHEW 11:28-30

Using very active scripture passages such as those above is helpful when you are having a very difficult time concentrating or controlling unnecessary thoughts. There will always be times when most of us will find using an active passage helpful. At other times, however, you might find that type of meditation too busy.

Another way to practice scripture meditation—one that is more quiet and more readily leads to simple contemplation—is to use a verse or two from the psalms or the prophetic writings such as Isaiah. Read the passage out loud, a phrase at a time. Following each phrase, close your eyes and *listen before moving on* to the next phrase. The silence between each phrase can be as long as you want. If your thoughts begin to wander during the silent times, just return to the phrase. You may repeat the same phrase as often as you like. Sometimes it is helpful to paraphrase the verse in your own language or repeat it in several different ways. If a certain word or phrase *touches* you, stay with that word or phrase until you feel like it is time to move on. You may feel a sense of awe at the greatness of God, somewhat like the way you might feel looking at a beautiful sunset, majestic mountains, or the power of the sea. You might be filled with a sense of God's love. There will most likely be no words to express how you feel, and you will be moved to silence. This is the beginning of contemplation. Stay with this silence and let it do its inner work.

Remember that the scripture text is not an assignment that you have to complete. If one word or thought draws you, it is more important to stay with that word or thought than it is to move on to something with less meaning just to finish the text. Scripture meditation is about falling in love with the One who has inspired these words, not learning more about the words themselves. It is also important to remember that whether we feel anything or not is not as important as our remembering that God is present and will fulfill the promise spoken through the prophet Jeremiah: *"When you search for me, you will find me; if you seek me with all your heart, I will let you find me."* [22]

As a monk, Martin Luther must have been schooled in this type of prayer. In his famous Letter to Peter the Barber,[23] Luther gave instructions on how to pray the Lord's Prayer. He told Peter to repeat each petition of the prayer slowly, leaving time for reflection after each petition. He then instructed Peter to respond with whatever prayer came to mind relating to that petition. Luther wrote that if the Holy Spirit began to speak to him, he should let go of his petitioning and listen because one word from the Holy Spirit is worth more than all his petitioning.

There are other ways of meditation that also can be very helpful. For example, reflecting on God in nature. To take intentional time to go for a walk, to sit on the beach, or just to gaze off one's backyard deck with the purpose of reflecting on the love and presence of God are ways of meditation that help one to be more in touch with God. Some find listening to good music is a way to open to God. Any creative effort from painting to pottery, from poetry to gardening can be a form of meditation that opens you to the divine within and around you.

Everyone is unique and will find different ways of meditation that will be helpful to them. The important thing is not how you meditate, but that you take time to be intentional about listening, reflecting, and pondering God's love, grace and provision for us through Jesus Christ. We begin the practice of scripture meditation as a way to know God more deeply. However, as we daily spend time in meditation, listening and responding to God, we will find that, not only are we growing in loving knowledge of God, we are also growing in loving knowledge of ourselves.

Reflection

Go to your sacred space and choose a short scripture passage from the psalms, a poetic writing such as the book of Isaiah, or a phrase or two from the New Testament for meditation. (See below for suggested texts.) Sit quietly and take several deep breaths. Imagine breathing in the Presence of the Holy Spirit and breathing out busy thoughts and worries. When you feel you are attentive, slowly read the scripture in the way suggested above.

Whatever happens during this time, pay attention to your feelings. Where are they inviting you to go inside? What are they drawing you to do or say? Respond to these feelings and stay with whatever is happening. It isn't necessary to finish the reading unless you feel drawn to it. When you are finished with your meditation, gently return and write the responses to your meditation in your journal.

Here are some suggested texts for this type of meditation. Psalms 139, 23, 62:1-2 ; Isaiah 43:1-5; Jeremiah 29:11-14 (remember to meditate on only a few verses at a time).

Solitude and Silence

For God alone my soul waits in silence,
my hope is from him . . .

PSALM 62:5

Be still and know that I am God . . .

PSALM 46:10

One of the most countercultural moves we can make is to spend time alone and in quiet. Silence and solitude are essential elements for the person who wants a more intimate *experience* of the presence of God. As in any love relationship, it is important to have time alone together in order to get beyond relating on a superficial level to relating with real depth and intimate communication. This is true in our relationship with God.

We may have known about Jesus before. We may have heard and read the Gospel stories about him. We may have been told things about him, but if we haven't been a praying person we will not have had the same kind of intimate personal encounter that happens in prayer. Hearing about someone from another source is never the same as getting to know that person personally. If we are quiet in our prayer and leave time to listen, God will communicate with us in ways that will help us to know God in an intimate and personal way. We will learn to recognize God by the peace and love we begin to experience even in the midst of difficult times.

In the 19th chapter of 1 Kings, we read of the prophet Elijah being under tremendous stress. There were threats against his life, he felt completely alone, and he was afraid. He traveled a day's journey into the wilderness and sat down under a tree. He was so depressed he asked God to take his life. It was in these dire circumstances that Elijah heard the "still small voice" of God in the silence. He couldn't hear God in the earthquake, or the wind, or the fire—only in silence.[24]

The same is true for us. Often we must get away from our surroundings to really begin to experience the presence of God even when our circumstances are very ordinary. This is even truer when we are surrounded by constant noise and busyness or when we are going through difficult times of depression, loneliness, or fear. In the place of solitude and silence we can begin to hear God and experience God's intimate, loving presence in our lives.

Many books on prayer written in earlier periods of Church history were written by monks or nuns who were cloistered in monasteries and living in silence. They spent their lives listening and in prayer with God. It may seem that their lifestyle wouldn't have anything to say to those of us who live in 21st-century Western culture; however, our culture is spiritually and psychologically starving for silence. Most of us live in constant noise pollution and don't even know it.

We live with the noise of cars, trucks, airplanes, sirens, radios, and TVs, to say nothing of the recorded music played in every store, every doctor's office, dentist's office, and restaurant, and which assaults us from the telephone every time we are left on hold. We are a plugged-in generation, constantly listening to iPods, MP3 players, CDs, or tapes.

Many of our church services also drown us in noise with praise bands blaring loud music in our *sanctuaries*. People seeking a spiritual life are often found plugged into earphones listening to Christian music or teaching tapes by some well-known Christian teacher. We are inundated with noise. Imagine how different it would be if the only sound one heard was the occasional bark of a dog.

We are also inundated with words through newspapers, magazines, road signs, billboards, the Internet, and so on. In my home, one of the hardest things I have to deal with is the amount of paper coming into the house in the form of advertising, catalogs, and the like. Most of us have no idea how filled we are with noise and words until we step away from them and spend some intentional time in silence.

Jesus taught us to incorporate a rhythm of activity and rest into our lives by the example of his life. Throughout the gospels we find Jesus surrounded by crowds crying out for his compassion and healing. He is under constant criticism from the religious and political authorities. The demands upon him seem endless and yet he frequently takes the time to withdraw to places of solitude to be alone with God. For example, Mark 1:35 says: "*In the morning, a great while before day, he rose and went out to a lonely place and there he prayed.*" He encouraged his disciples to do the same. In Mark 6:31, Jesus tells them: "*Come away by your selves to a lonely place and rest awhile. For many were coming and going and they had no leisure even to eat."*

The early Christians felt they had to get away from the culture of their time in order to seriously seek God. In her collection *Sayings of the Desert Fathers*, Benedicta Ward states that society "was regarded as a shipwreck from which each single individual man had to swim for his life. . . These were men who believed that to let oneself drift along, passively accepting the tenets and values of what they knew as society, was purely and simply a disaster."[25] They took seriously Jesus' call to leave all and follow him.[26]

Today people are trying to juggle their own schedules of work and other responsibilities plus the schedules of their busy children. Many remark to me that they have no idea where they could possibly find the time to pay attention to their spiritual lives. Probably the most difficult hindrance to spiritual life today is simply finding the space and time to tend seriously to your relationship with God.

Obviously, prayer and meditation take time. It takes a conscious effort to find a small space to fit them in. The serious God seeker has to be very deliberate about this, especially when you are just beginning to deepen your prayer. A good way to begin is to make an appointment with God, mark it on your calendar as you would any other appointment—and keep it. If we make an appointment with any one else, we are careful to keep it. If we are meeting a friend for coffee we wouldn't think of just not showing up. I often tell people in spiritual formation that their most difficult spiritual discipline will be "showing up!"

Evaluate your days (and nights) and try to see spaces that are used for something else that isn't essential such as reading the newspaper or watching television. When my children were little, I found that getting up a littler earlier than they did was a good way to find a quiet place for myself. Even today, I find that if I don't take the time in the morning for prayer and meditation, I will have a hard time getting it once the daily schedule starts.

It is helpful to have a space somewhere in your home that is your quiet corner. It can be as simple as a particular chair. By using the same space all the time, the space itself becomes sacred and an aid to focusing on God. When all our children were home, I chose a corner in my dining room. I would often put a candle, a cross, flowers or other religious object there to help me focus my attention on God. In warm weather, a place outdoors can become that special place and all of nature the icons that will point you to God.

Reflection

Find a place in your home that can be used for a sacred space, a trysting place with God. Be creative in arranging it with things that will call you to prayer and open your heart to God. You can use a candle, a picture, or a plant as a focus point. Remember this can be simply a corner of a room that is used for other things. Consecrate that space to God to prepare it for future times of meeting with the Beloved. Before moving on with this book, create your sacred space, tell your family or anyone else you are living with what you are doing and why, and then spend a few moments there feeling the silence and opening yourself to God's presence to you and within you.

Retreats

. . . Arise my love, my fair one,
and come away.

SONG OF SOLOMON 2:10

It takes time to learn how to be alone and silent. In the early stages, it is very helpful to go to a retreat center where you can experience a planned retreat in an atmosphere of silence. For many, it will be easier to get accustomed to being alone with God when they are together with others who are doing the same thing. Also, it is easier to stay attentive to God in solitude when there are no family, work, telephones, televisions or other distractions to grab your attention.

Being a very gregarious and extroverted person, I found retreats essential to learning how to slow down and listen. Some people will say that extroverts don't do well with silent retreats but I disagree because of my own experience. Admittedly, when I first started going on retreat, I did find it difficult. It was culture shock. I was so accustomed to noise, busyness, and talking that I was blown away by simply being in silence. As an extrovert, when I was with others, everything I thought or imagined would come pouring out of my mouth with little reflection. Making small talk was the norm.

During silent retreats, however, I discovered that there was no need to pay attention to, or make small talk with, other people. We were able to just "be" in our own thoughts. We were together in silence. I actually found it to be a relief not to have to be "up" for anything; I could just relax. In time I came to know the depth of community that takes place in and through silence.

Getting accustomed to the silence of a retreat takes time. It took me half of my first retreat to quiet down inside and be in a position to hear my inner thoughts or even to notice that they were there. At first I felt like I was wasting my time. I thought I could have been home doing things with my family to say nothing of all the never-ending household chores. As much as I questioned the value of taking time away, however, it was the beginning of a life transforming habit that has probably saved my life in many ways.

After attending several retreats, I began to carry the retreat experience home by planning daily quiet time. I found that more and more I depended on periods of silence to keep my awareness of God present in my life. When it was possible, I would work and drive my car in silence. Some days I would take "a vow of silence" for a part of the day. I would not answer the phone, play music, or speak.

I began to cherish my times of silence. They seemed to give my life more substance and grounding than I had ever felt before. I gradually became better at not overextending myself with activities and people. I also became more focused on whatever I had to do. My awareness of God grew and deepened. In time I found that the retreat experience was no longer culture shock but an extension of what I was experiencing in my daily life. This did not happen overnight, but took time—as do all things related to spiritual life.

Reflection

A simple way to practice solitude and silence is to learn to *shut it off.* You can add this practice to your spiritual practice of *showing up.* Shut off the radio, the TV, and the CD player. Try driving your car in silence—with no cell phone. When you have a period of time at home or in your office alone, work in silence. If possible, unplug the telephone for a few hours. Don't check e-mail for an afternoon. Go for a walk alone and in silence. Take a simple vow of silence for a certain period of time.

Remember that when we fill our minds with words those words and thoughts will surface during periods of silence. Try not reading the newspaper or magazines on some days. Pay attention to what goes on in your head and ask yourself how helpful or necessary are the words that are filling your mind. If possible, you may want to plan a short retreat. This can be a day or even half a day away at a retreat center or other quiet place. These are simple spiritual practices that can help you to become silent inside and begin to notice your interior life and relationship with God.

Practicing the
Presence of God

. . . so that they would search for God
and perhaps grope for him and perhaps find him—
though indeed he is not far from each one of us.
For "in him we live and move and have our being" . . .

ACTS 17:27-28

It is difficult to remember that we are children of God and that God is with us at all times. We may feel close to God during meditation, in nature, through music or in church. We often lose that sense of closeness, however, when we are busy with work, relationships, or play. Other responsibilities, people, places, or things crowd out our desire for God and we may find that we are no longer listening or paying attention to the inner Spirit that guides our way.

An ancient spiritual discipline that can help us remember God in the midst of ordinary life is the *practice of the presence of God*. There are several ways to practice the presence of God (some of which I will talk about here), but each of us can find ways to notice God's presence that work best for ourselves. Just as we learn to meditate and pray with scripture in ways unique to ourselves, so will we find ways to pay attention and notice God's presence and action in all of life that are unique to ourselves. The point isn't to be successful with a certain method. The point is to be intentional about being open to God no matter what we are doing or what is going on around us.

Just as active prayer is most helpful in the beginning of our journey, so will a more active way be most helpful when you are first practicing the presence of God. Frank Laubach, in his little book, *The Game of Minutes*[27], tells of imagining God with him moment by moment in everything he did. He imagined God moving his fingers as he typed his manuscripts and accompanying him as he walked to the village or went about his work. He tells of how this practice transformed both his life and the way people responded to him as he went about the village.

Brother Lawrence, a Carmelite monk of the fourteenth century, in his famous classic, *Practicing the Presence of God*,[28] tells of God being with him among the pots and pans of the monastery kitchen and of how he often felt closer to God there than at times of organized worship.

The Desert Mothers and Fathers of the fourth and fifth centuries, the famous monks on Mt. Athos in Greece, and the Russian *staretz*, or hermits, left us a spiritual legacy with the Jesus Prayer. This prayer has been used throughout the centuries and has come into popularity again in recent history. This prayer, based on scripture,[29] involves the constant repetition of the words: "Lord Jesus Christ, Son of God, have mercy on me, a sinner." The Jesus Prayer has been used in various forms, from the complete verse above, to the shorter, "Jesus, have mercy," or simply the name,

"Jesus." I have found the latter to be very helpful in returning my focus to my Center. Sometimes when I feel particularly tense simply saying Jesus' name in rhythm with my breathing causes me to relax and focus.

The short book *The Way of a Pilgrim*[30] tells of an anonymous Russian pilgrim's experience with the Jesus Prayer. After hearing a sermon about Paul's admonition to "pray without ceasing," [31] the pilgrim sets out to learn what this means. After confronting many other Christians with his questions about praying ceaselessly, he finally meets a hermit who tells him about the Jesus Prayer. The hermit tells the pilgrim to say the prayer thousands of times a day. At first he repeats the prayer over and over verbally, then he begins repeating the prayer in his mind. In time, he practices synchronizing the mental repetition of the prayer with his heartbeat or with his breathing. He lives the prayer. You may find it interesting to read of his experience with the Jesus Prayer; for me, the most important thing he said about his experience is that after a time the prayer began to pray itself within his heart.

In the beginning of any prayer practice, one has to apply oneself to the practice. It takes effort and discipline. But the fruit of this effort is that eventually "the prayer prays itself." In other words, the prayer enters both our conscious and subconscious and goes on quite naturally as we go about our daily business. Not only does the prayer say itself, it eventually becomes like a sixth sense, an openness to the Spirit that functions almost effortlessly alongside, and just as naturally as, all our other senses.

In my own experience of practicing the presence of God, I have used some very simple and practical ways of reminding myself to turn to God all day long. When I went up the stairs I thought of ascending into God. When I went down the stairs I thought of descending into God. When I washed my hands I would think of being forgiven. When I drove my car, every telephone pole became a cross reminding me to turn to God. Every tree, flower, or blade of grass moved me to reach out to God who created them (and who created me). The more I thought of God, the more I would think of God, until I didn't need to think of God. Eventually my inner person seemed to be naturally open to God underlying everything I did without any mental effort on my part.

In time, as your experience of God's presence within becomes more natural, you may find that simply recalling that Presence and intentionally turning toward Christ within will bring you back to a simple awareness of God without the need for words or images. Your inner spirit becomes like the needle of a compass that turns north naturally at all times. This continual simple awareness all day long prepares you for your set aside time for prayer and meditation. It seems this practice helps keep the mind from becoming overly cluttered and busy and enables you to enter the quiet of prayer more easily.

At this point one could ask: "Is all this necessary?" Some traditions might say: "We don't have to make all this effort. We receive everything by grace without works." That is true, but we are talking about *experiencing* the gifts that come from grace. We are talking about a deepening *awareness* of God's gift of presence. We are talking about *opening* ourselves to the gracious, freely given, transforming power and presence of Holy Spirit within us. To the degree that we are able to live our lives with a continuing awareness of God and the gifts of God, our lives are enriched and enhanced. It is for us, not for God, and it is worth it. Just like anything else in our life that is worth something, we need to put forth a little effort.

The end result of spiritual practice is that we train our unruly thought life to be open to God. We learn by practice to open our inner person so God can get through our toughness and breathe the fresh wind of the Spirit into all of our lives. This takes nothing away from grace. It is because of the generous grace and love of God for us that we want to be—and are enabled to be—open to God's gifts and aware of God's presence and guidance in all of life.

Reflection

Today try saying the Jesus Prayer as often as you think of it all day long: "Lord, Jesus Christ, Son of God, have mercy on me, a sinner." You may use a shortened form of the prayer if you want. At the end of the day, think over your day and see how it went. You may want to journal about your experience, and you may want to begin practicing the Jesus Prayer every day.

Consciousness *Examen*

You desire truth in the inward being;
Therefore teach me wisdom in my secret heart.

PSALM 4:2

Another ancient practice that is helpful in our spiritual deepening is what is called (from Latin) an *examen* at the end of the day. This is a very helpful practice to add to the rhythm of your day, especially if your daily quiet time is in the morning.

Our desire is to be open to God in all of our day to day life. We want to enjoy the abundant love and grace that God has lavished upon us through Christ. As said before, we often lose our connection with God amid the busyness and stress of all the activities and responsibilities of our days. By deliberately attending to how connected we have felt to God throughout our day, however, we become aware of what causes us to lose our focus and what helps us to stay attentive to God in the midst of our days. In our prayer, we can ask God to help us with those times that cloud our consciousness and lead to God-forgetfulness.

Every day brings with it issues and concerns that require decisions and responses from us. Some of these cause reactions that come from places deep within and have nothing to do with the issue at hand. Often these reactions are painful and bring up old feelings of guilt, shame, or fear. We don't know why we say the things we do or feel the way we feel when confronted with certain situations. These reactions can be barriers or stumbling blocks to our relationship with others as well as our relationship with God. By paying attention to these feelings and taking a little time to examine them and open them to the light of God's wisdom, we soon begin to notice what causes the reaction and, in time, what is the hidden reason for the feelings. When we realize what these subconscious reasons are, we also begin to be healed of them as we bring them to the unconditional love and forgiveness of God.

Taking time at the end of the day for an examination of our consciousness also helps us in our discernment regarding decisions and choices that we need to make. Often when we are confronted with a decision or choice, whether it be as big as a new job or as simple as whether or not to attend a certain event, if we are paying attention we will notice a change in our inner atmosphere. These inner feelings can be life giving such as joy, excitement and positive anticipation or negative such as dread or heaviness. The feelings can draw us in or push us away. Internal changes like this can happen in simple moments, even during a conversation. They are often a way God uses to show us what are God's invitations and what are not for us at this time. We only need to learn to recognize them.

The consciousness *examen* need not be cumbersome or time consuming. Granted, sometimes there will be issues that cause you to spend more time examining yourself, but on a daily basis it can be as simple as just mentally thinking back over your day and asking where you felt near to God and where you felt drawn away from, or forgetful of, God present in your daily experience. My own practice is simple. As I lie down in bed at night, I shut my eyes and mentally run through my day before I go to sleep. This way I can pay attention to what were the significant feelings that were either life giving or upsetting and ask God to show me why.

During your *examen*, you may have feelings that require forgiveness for yourself or others. Bringing all these things into the light of God's love and forgiveness helps us to clear the slate of our day so, as the book of Proverbs says, "... *when you lie down, your sleep will be sweet.*" [32]

Martin Luther tells us that we are born anew every day. That which happened yesterday is over and the new has come. Daily the old false self is dying and the new self in Christ is being born.[33] The consciousness *examen* at the end of the day helps us to realize this great gift of continual new life in Christ.

Reflection

Make a note for yourself and put it by your bedside reminding you of the consciousness *examen*. Try it for a few nights and record your experience and feelings about it in your journal. Pay attention to how helpful it is as you go about your days.

Creating a Rule of Life

Devote yourselves to prayer,
keeping alert in it with thanksgiving.

COLOSSIANS 4:2

A Rule is a simple structure that one chooses as a *framework* to help *guide* one's life and spiritual growth. Religious orders all have a Rule that they live by. The most famous of these is probably the Benedictine Rule that was established hundreds of years before the Reformation.[34] Many religious orders today use the Benedictine Rule, as do many lay people who desire to live a more committed and faithful Christian life. In creating your own Rule, what I am suggesting will in no way compare to the richness or detail of the Benedictine Rule but will, hopefully, help you fulfill *your own desires* for a deeper spiritual life.

In our modern society, words like rule aren't very popular. Many of us grew up with harsh discipline and legalism either at home, school or in our church life. Because of this we are afraid of anything that sounds like a return to that rigid way of life. I am not suggesting that. A Rule is simply *practices* that we have found helpful and *choose* to use as a guide for our spiritual lives. Our

Rule is not a rigid law that we have to do or that God is demanding of us.

In all other aspects of life we think nothing of planning towards a goal or putting forth some effort to gain a desired end. For example, if one wants to be a doctor or an engineer, one plans for years of education involving long hours of disciplined study and practice. A good athlete or musician practices hours every day even after they become proficient. For some reason, when we think of our spiritual lives we hesitate to talk about discipline or effort for fear of becoming legalistic. That very hesitancy often keeps us from developing the kind of spiritual life we ourselves long for.

A Rule of Life should be simple. It should be something that works for us in our uniqueness. It is a structure for life that can help us stay connected to the Source of Life. Sometimes I like to think of my spiritual life as a climbing vine that needs a trellis to attach itself to in order to grow. Without the trellis the plant just keeps falling down on itself and makes no progress. Our Rule of Life is like a trellis that supports our spiritual life as we grow.

A Rule of Life also gives us rhythms of prayer and work that help us retain our focus on God while helping us be open to God throughout the day. It is also something that encourages us through irregular times like when relatives are visiting or we are on vacation. Often during times like these it is easy to get out of the routine of prayer, meditation, or keeping one's journal. When you have your Rule it is easier to pick up and start again. A Rule is something that one usually keeps in ordinary time and as soon as time returns to the ordinary one can easily return to the Rule.

A Rule is also something that is portable. You can take it with you anywhere, just like a suitcase. When you are committed to your Rule, it becomes a habit that you do in some form or another wherever you are. Serious runners take their athletic shoes with them wherever they go. Whenever it works out, the runner can always get in a run. When you are committed to your Rule, wherever you are, you will be encouraged perhaps to take a meditative walk, or find a few moments for prayer or spiritual reading.

What is important is to let the Rule be a helpful tool for you and not something that drives you or makes you feel guilty if you don't follow it exactly every day. It is your Rule that you choose and you can change it to fit your needs as your needs change. It is not something that you have to do to be acceptable to God. We can look at Jesus' life as an example. He sought out times when he could be alone with God whenever he had a chance. Sometimes it was early in the morning. Other times it was at night, and he often withdrew during the day, even when the crowds pressed in on him—but he was not rigid. There were times when he gave up his time alone to serve the people who came to him. We need to be that flexible with ourselves.

To adopt a spiritual Rule is simply to decide how you want to live out your relationship with God and which spiritual practices will help you. For some reason we humans have a tendency to make everything guilt producing. When we commit ourselves to a Rule this is even truer. Remember, your Rule is just that—*your* Rule. It is something you create to help yourself be more attentive to God. It will change from time to time depending on your circumstances. Maybe we could say that a Rule is something we aspire to, that we are always living into. Just remember that a Rule it is not a law that God has mandated. This is your Rule, created by you to help your spiritual growth.

A simple Rule could look something like this:

Rule of Life

In response to the lavish love of God poured out for me, I choose these spiritual practices to help me be more open to God's work in my life so that I might appropriate and enjoy the grace given to me as well as live a more Christ-centered and Christlike life in the world . . . with God's help.

Daily Quiet time: 20 minutes or more (this should include some form of scripture meditation and silence)

Examen: 5 minutes at end of day before sleep

Practice the Presence of God: Each day, as often as you think of it, with the goal of it becoming an interior habit.

Physical Exercise: Walk or run (outside or on a treadmill), do strength training—or just take the dog for a long walk. Exercise should be done in a meditative way that keeps your thoughts open to the inspiration of the Spirit.

Journal keeping: As detailed or as simple as you choose, but practice some form of reflecting on and recording developments in your spiritual thoughts and experiences; note how they are affecting your human development, your relationships, your peace, love, joy, etc.

Family and Friends: Spend quality time with family and touch base with a personal friend every week.

Fun: Do something fun!

This is a very basic Rule, but you can include other practices that you think would be helpful to you. My own rule includes the above with a more extended time for morning meditation and silence. I also read a short Daily Office.[35] I write in my journal a few times a week, walk daily, practice the presence of God, and do a simple *examen* before I go to sleep. I take retreat time periodically and see a spiritual director every other month. I retired a few years ago so I could concentrate my time on writing and art. In order to accomplish this, and not just drift through my days, I include the discipline of writing every day if possible and giving time to watercolor painting. I keep a spiritual book going to stimulate my hunger for God and expand my knowledge of spiritual things. I also read a good best seller and listen to good music to keep me in touch with all of life.

You will notice this is very fluid and all but your basic practices will change as you grow and change. Being attentive to God and spending time in silence and meditation will help you to notice what is missing and what practices God might be inviting you to include at different times. Never let your Rule be guilt producing and legalistic. It should be simply a grace-full way to help you realize your own dreams.

Reflection

Create a Rule of Life for yourself. Set aside some time to reflect on the spiritual practices that you have read about so far. Which of these do you feel especially drawn to? Remember, what is important is not what particular style of prayer you are doing at any given time in your life. What is important is that you pray, that you "show up," and incorporate some time for silence, solitude and reflection into your daily life.

What are the goals you have for your spiritual life? What do want in your relationship with God? How you are going to make that happen? What spiritual practices do you want to include that will help your dream be realized? You might think about your life, what your days look like and ask yourself what is missing. This also can be a clue as to what spiritual practices you might want to include.

The Contemplative Journey

. . . What no eye has seen,
nor ear heard,
nor the human heart conceived,
what God has prepared for those who love him.

1 CORINTHIANS 2:9

Remember, we are on a journey, a journey from feeling separation and distance from God to experiencing oneness or union with God. This is normal spiritual deepening. In the beginning of this book, I talked about how, after we have been spiritually active and praying petitions and intercessions for a long time, our prayer can become dry and without feeling. When our spiritual life has consisted primarily of activity and the saying of prayers, God invites us to go deeper. Let's recap what you can expect on the journey.

At first, the invitation to greater depth comes in a negative way in that our spiritual life seems to dry up. This is a time of transition from more active forms of prayer to more silent, reflective, contemplative forms of prayer. This transition comes as a surprise to many because it hasn't been discussed much in the Protestant tradition. What I have tried to do with this book is to give you both suggestions for new ways to pray when your prayer has become dry and suggestions for spiritual practices that will support your deepening spiritual life. These practices will help you move through this change from active to more contemplative prayer.

Changes in our spiritual life will continue as we deepen spiritually. As we spend time in solitude and silence, as we pray with the scriptures, and as we are faithful to other spiritual practices, we become more open to God's unconditional love that is always being lavished upon us. We grow in loving knowledge of God and ourselves, and we grow in our ability to love. We begin to realize in a greater way how precious and unique we are. This is not something we have to strive for or try to make happen. It is the natural result of our spending intentional time with God. The more we realize that we are loved unconditionally and beyond our comprehension, the more we open ourselves to God. Just as in our human relationships, we let our guard down. The inner walls that have formed a protective barrier around our hearts come down. As a result, we begin to have a greater experience of closeness or intimacy with God.

This experience of intimacy and closeness will affect the way we pray. In the beginning, I spoke of our relationship with God as being similar to our other interpersonal relationships. Just as we grow in intimacy with someone we love by spending time together and sharing all of our lives, so it is with God. As we get past the getting acquainted part of our relationship with God, we are like two people deeply in love who desire times just to be alone together, times when words and actions are neither necessary nor helpful.

When this begins to happen in our relationship with God, our prayer begins to change. At first, you may have found meditation on scripture or other forms of active meditation to be very helpful in drawing you into a quiet time with God. In time, however, when you begin your quiet time, you may discover that using scripture or other types of active reflection make you feel as though you are stepping back from God rather than drawing close. Eventually, when you come to your prayer time, you may find that you just want to sit there, *saying* nothing, *doing* nothing. Simple silence is more compelling than any activity.

You may experience the same dynamic with all of the spiritual practices that you have found helpful in the past. You may feel a deep sense of Presence as you go about your daily routine, but as soon as you try to actively practice the presence of God you find yourself feeling more distant from God. Or you may have found attending a Bible study or prayer group helpful in your spiritual life but now you feel an aversion rather than an attraction to such activities. You may have enjoyed being with your spiritual friends and sharing your experiences of God or with scripture and the like. Now you find you would simply rather be alone. You no longer desire to talk about your relationship with God—you simply want to rest in God, to *be* in God.

When you seek advice for your "condition" from your peers, or even spiritual leaders, they may tell you that you need to pray more or study the Bible more. They might suggest that you may have done something in your past that you haven't repented of, that you have some unconfessed sin that you are guilty of. The more you try to heed such advice, however, the more your "condition" worsens. You begin to feel that maybe you were never really a Christian at all or, at the very least, never a very spiritual person. It seems like the spiritual life you once enjoyed and were drawn to has died.

This "dark night" is one of the most difficult times in the spiritual life. Unless you have good guidance to help you through this time, it can be devastating. It seems like you, who may have been the most serious God seeker, are going backwards rather than forward. It seems that you have lost your desire for God and the spiritual life.

It is hard to imagine that this is a time of maturing and deepening—but it is. This is actually a time when God is inviting you into a more immediate, intimate, and contemplative relationship. This is the time in your relationship with God when you leave your dependence on feelings, thoughts, and emotions behind and live in naked trust in the presence, love, and grace of God.

In our pragmatic, utilitarian, rational culture, we have learned little about the real contemplative experience spoken of in the classic writings of the ancient mystics. Teaching about prayer has been reduced to the practical aspects of intercession and petition, and our relationship with God has been reduced to *doing* things that we hope will accomplish what we think might be God's will.

When one experiences contemplative awareness, however, one can no longer rely on self-effort. Before we may have chosen particular spiritual practices that have been helpful but now we find our spiritual life is truly in the hands of God. We begin to realize that our spiritual journey is not about us but about God. It is all grace. God chooses us. God invites us to prayer. God enables our spiritual practices. Only God can heal us and make us whole.

Only God knows where we are going and what lies ahead for us. We begin to realize that it is only in loving knowledge of God that we know God at all. We cannot know God through our intellect or reason. Scripture tells us: *"What no eye has seen, nor ear heard nor the heart conceived, what God has prepared beforehand for those that love God—these things God has revealed to us through the Spirit; for the Spirit searches everything, even the depths of God."* [36]

Loving knowledge of God goes beyond our comprehension, beyond our theologies and doctrines. The experience of loving and being loved by God fulfills our hearts desire more than we can think or imagine. We realize that nothing can separate us from the love of God.[37] Jesus tells us that we shall be one with God as he is, and one with each other.[38] We begin to experience a sense of oneness with God and all creation. Our heart becomes like a cup constantly being filled to overflowing. Even when there is no sense awareness of God's presence or love, there still seems to be an underlying simple *knowing* that is beyond emotion thought, and feeling—a *knowing* that undergirds our life.

The question is how does one pray during this time of transition? How does one pay attention and continue to be open to God? The answer, I believe, is to pray in whatever ways make sense to you, trusting that God is leading you through your prayer to a deeper awareness of—and experience of—God's transforming presence. Be willing to leave old ways of prayer and spiritual practice behind when they no longer seem to work. Trust that God is leading you to new ways of prayer and practice.

Be willing to leave the safety of your verbal prayer and active meditation and go with your heart into the stillness where God is known in silence and in love. Remember, however, that even though your heart desires to sit in silence, your mind won't always cooperate. There will be times when the distractions and worries of your busy life will fill and trouble your mind when you want to become quiet. Should that happen, simply observe your breathing for a few moments until you begin to feel centered and then return to the silence. Go back to observing your breathing for a few moments each time you find your mind distracted, returning to the silence when you are ready.

You may also find it helpful to choose a simple word that you can use when thoughts or feelings invade the silence. Choose a one or two syllable word that is life giving to you and into which you can place all your love and longing for God. It may be as simple as God or Yahweh, Christ, love, joy, peace, etc. Synchronize your word with your breathing, mentally repeating it with each inhalation and exhalation. I have used the name of Jesus, breathing in on the first syllable and out on the second.

If distracting thoughts or feelings come and disturb your silence, in sync with your breathing, slowly begin to say your word, either in your mind or softly out loud, to push away the thoughts and leave you centered in God. When you feel centered again, leave your word and return to the silence. Come back to your word whenever you need to. Your word may change from time to time depending on what is going on in your life, but let that word express your love and longing for God; simply let it surface within you—and lead you to silence.

Remember, contemplative prayer takes place in the heart, in the center of your soul. It doesn't take place in your mind. As you sit in silence you will become aware that your thoughts are no more important than the cars driving by on the street or the birds flying about in the sky. You don't have to run and look at (or think about) every car or bird. They are just there. In the same way, thoughts, feelings, and images may float by in your mind while your heart is engaged in communion with God. You don't have to pay attention to them. Let them come and let them go.

Communion with God takes place in the heart. If it is a very busy time in your life and your mind is particularly active, simply enter prayer by breathing deeply and imagine following your breathe to the center of your soul. To repeat what was said above, stay there in the quiet, and if thoughts invade, simply return to your breath or begin repeating the sacred word that you have chosen.

Contemplative prayer is about learning to *be* and not to *do*; it is learning to receive God's grace and be filled with the Spirit who transforms us into the image of Christ.[39] As we take time for solitude, silence, and prayer, we find that we aren't separating ourselves from the world but that we take the world with us in our hearts when we enter into the silence where God is known in love.

As we grow and deepen in our relationship with God, we become our truest and best self, and we engage those around us and in the world in new ways. William Johnston quotes the Catholic theologian William Lonergan in saying that "Religious experience at its roots is experience of an unconditional and unrestricted being in love. But what we are in love with remains something that we have to find out." Johnston goes on to say that this means that what makes religious meditation religious (as opposed to secular forms of meditation practiced for the development of human potential) is the dimension of love. "This is a love that springs from the depths of the spirit, from the fine point or centre of the soul, from the core of the being where men and women are most truly themselves."[40]

As with so many things in the spiritual life, it is a paradox that as we learn to *be* in Love, we also become more Christlike in the world. As we seek God, we are seeking not only for our own personal healing and transformation but for the healing and transformation of the world. The world is waiting for us.[41]

Reflection

In your quiet time, sit in silence, waiting on God, using breath prayer to stay attentive. If your mind wanders, simply take a deep breath, following the breath in to the deep place inside yourself. Stay focused on that space, paying attention to your breathing. Return there whenever your mind becomes active. If it is more helpful to use a simple word or the name of Jesus to bring your thoughts back to the silence, be free to do that. Spend twenty minutes or more in this way of practicing silence. When you are finished, gently return to the present moment.

Write your reflections in your journal. It is important to be honest in your reflections. If the silence seems flat or boring write about that. Even the emptiness of dry prayer will draw you into the depths of God that go beyond feeling, thought or emotion. Sometimes, as you write, you will uncover layers beneath the initial feelings that give insight into your soul. At other times you may find that there are no words to express what you have experienced. During these times it may be helpful to write poetry, draw a picture, or express yourself in some other form of art. There are many ways to express our love relationship with God.

Spiritual Direction

. . . Were not our hearts burning within us
while he was talking to us on the road,
while he was opening the scriptures to us?

As I mentioned earlier, I have had a spiritual director to support and guide my own contemplative journey. A spiritual director is a person who has been carefully trained in the skills of helping others with their prayer and spiritual life. He or she will be a person of deep prayer, a fellow traveler on the contemplative journey, well grounded in both scripture and the spiritual traditions and practices of the church.

A spiritual director is a good listener who can help you discern what God is doing in your life. A spiritual director can suggest appropriate spiritual practices, encourage you in following them, and hold you accountable. A good spiritual director is a wise guide and a gentle truth-teller.

Not everyone will have this type of spiritual director. However, as your prayer becomes more interior a lot of unconscious psychological debris that may have been hidden for years may begin to surface. Although the surfacing of this debris is a path to healing and wholeness, it is also a path frequently fraught with emotional and spiritual danger. At such times, I would strongly suggest having a spiritual director, or perhaps even a therapist, to listen and help you process, and gain freedom from, these old memories and their associated feelings and emotions. At the very least, you should have a mature spiritual friend whom you trust to share your experience with and to seek counsel from.

For me, having a spiritual director keeps me open and honest and helps me stay true to the spiritual path I have chosen. My spiritual director reminds me of the invitations and opportunities I have received from God when I have let them pass unacknowledged. And my spiritual director reminds me of God's unconditional love for my unique self when I forget.

Reflection

Spend some time thinking about who might be a good spiritual friend for you, someone you trust well enough to share your contemplative journey with, someone who has the spiritual maturity to listen and understand. You want a friend who can help you discern what God is doing in your life, someone who can encourage you in your spiritual practice, someone who will be a truth-teller and help to keep you honest and humble in your journey into God.

If there is such a person in your life, approach them and begin a conversation. If you both feel comfortable with where the conversation goes (be honest with each other) you will have a spiritual friend to walk with you through both the highs and lows of your spiritual journey.

A Final Word

But you beloved,
Build yourselves up on your most holy faith;
Pray in the Holy Spirit;
Keep yourselves in the love of God;
Look forward to the mercy of our Lord Jesus Christ
That leads to eternal life.

JUDE 20-21

Contemplative prayer is not a destination. *Being* contemplative is a way of life. I would suggest that a contemplative way of life is one in which we *habitually* give ourselves time for solitude and silence, for listening and paying attention to God's activity in our lives. The particular forms of prayer you use will change as you are healed and transformed from the inside out. As inner healing takes place, your prayer will become more quiet and you will desire to sit in God's presence without activity, words, or images. This is a very natural and profound part of spiritual growth.

In contemplative prayer, we do not "arrive," rather we continue to journey into deeper layers of silence in prayer. The important thing is to be faithful, to *show up* for prayer even when the silence becomes deafening. As you continue, you will find that the scripture is true: *From ages past no one has heard, nor ear has perceived, no eye has seen any God besides you, who works for those who wait for him.*[42]

Notes

1. Ephesians 2:10
2. Psalm 139:13-18
3. Psalm 46:10; Mark 6:31
4. Isaiah 6:5
5. Psalm 46:10
6. John 14:15-23
7. John 15:9-15
8. Matthew 28:20
9. John 17:20-26
10. Acts 17:28
11. Isaiah 43:4
12. Jeremiah 31:3
13. John 14:15-23
14. Romans 8:15, 16, 26
15. 2 Corinthians 3:18
16. Romans 8:9, 15-16
17. Ephesians 2:8
18. John 38–44
19. Philippians 3:13

20. *Teresa of Avila*, Vol. 1, 2, 3 (Washington D.C.: ICS, 1979).

21. Galatians 5:6, cf. 1 John 4:7-8

22. Jeremiah 29:13

23. Martin Luther. "Letter to Peter the Barber" in *Luther's Works*, Vol. 43 (Minneapolis: Augsburg Fortress, 1968).

24. 1 Kings 19:11-12

25. Benedicta Ward, trans. *The Sayings of the Desert Fathers* (London & Oxford: Mowbrays, 1975), 8.

26. Luke 5:11

27. Frank Laubach. "The Game with Minutes" in *Practicing His Presence*, Library of Spiritual Classics Vol. 1 (Jacksonville, FL: Seed Sowers, 1973).

28. Brother Laurence, "The Practice of the Presence of God" in *Practicing His Presence*, Library of Spiritual Classics (Jacksonville, FL: Seed Sowers, 1973).

29. Luke 18:39

30. Anonymous. *The Way of the Pilgrim*, Walter J. Ciszek and Helen Bacovcin, trans. (New York, Doubleday Image, 1978).

31. 1 Thessalonians 5:17

32. Proverbs 3:24

33. 2 Corinthians 5:17

34. Esther de Waal. *Seeking God: The Way of St. Benedict* (Collegeville: Liturgical, 1984).

35. In recent years I have used *The Divine Hours* by Phyllis Tickle, Doubleday, 2001. Even though I spend more time in silence, I like the structure of praying the psalms. I feel a connection with the whole church everyday through this type of liturgical prayer.

36. 1 Corinthians 2:9-10

37. Romans 8:38-39

38. John 17:22-23

39. 2 Corinthians 3:18

40. William Johnston. *Being In Love* (New York: Harper and Row, 1989), 12.

41. Romans 8:19

42. Isaiah 64:4